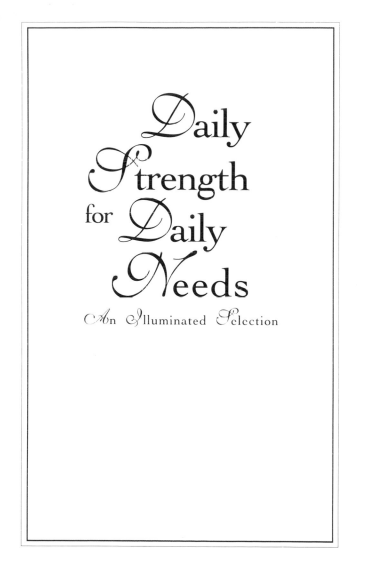

Daily Strength for Daily Needs

An Illuminated Selection

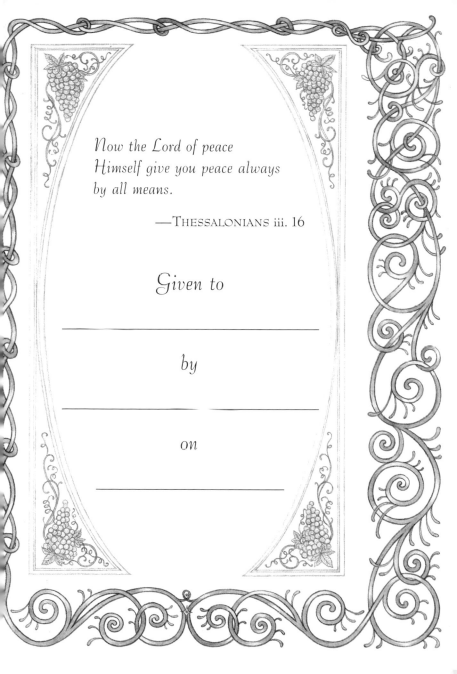

Now the Lord of peace
Himself give you peace always
by all means.

—Thessalonians iii. 16

Given to

_____

by

_____

on

_____

*W*atercolors by
Claudia Karabaic Sargent

*S*elected by
Peg Streep

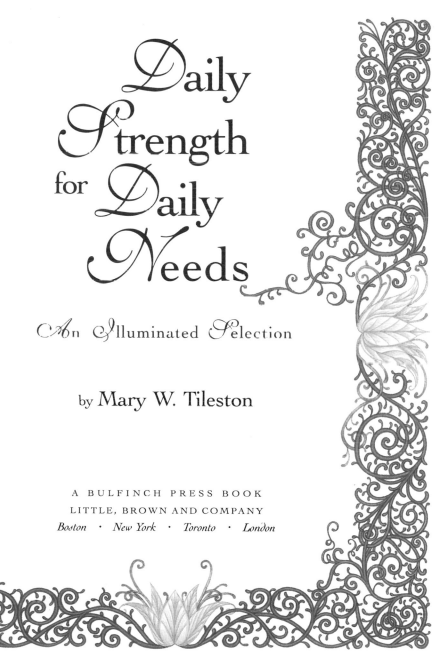

Daily Strength for Daily Needs

An Illuminated Selection

by Mary W. Tileston

A BULFINCH PRESS BOOK
LITTLE, BROWN AND COMPANY
Boston · *New York* · *Toronto* · *London*

For my mother and father,
with love and gratitude for their
countless gifts to me

—C.K.S.

Compilation copyright © 1994 by Peg Streep
Illustrations copyright © 1994 by Claudia Karabaic Sargent
Text copyright by Mary W. Tileston

First Edition
Text design by Dede Cummings / IPA

LIBRARY OF CONGRESS CATALOGING-IN-PUBLICATION DATA

Daily strength for daily needs. An illuminated selection. /
[compiled by] Mary W. Tileston ; selected by Peg Streep ;
illustrated by Claudia Karabaic Sargent. — 1st ed.
    p. cm.
  "A Bulfinch Press book."
  ISBN 0-8212-2073-X
  1. Devotional calendars.   I. Tileston, Mary Wilder, 1843–
1934. II. Streep, Peg.   III. Sargent, Claudia Karabaic.   IV.
Title.
BV4810.D258   1993
242'.2 — dc20   93-39923

Bulfinch Press is an imprint and trademark of Little, Brown and
Company (Inc.)

Published simultaneously in Canada by Little, Brown and
Company (Canada) Limited

PRINTED IN ITALY

O come, let us sing unto the Lord; let us make a joyful noise to the rock of our salvation.

Let us come before His presence with thanksgiving, and make a joyful noise unto Him with psalms.

For the Lord is a great God, and a great King above all gods.

In His hand are the deep places of the earth: the strength of the hills is His also.

The sea is His, and He made it: and His hands formed the dry land.

O come, let us worship and bow down: let us kneel before the Lord our maker.

For he is our God; and we are the people of His pasture, and the sheep of His hand.

—PSALM xcv. 1–7

FAITH

The kingdom of God is within you.

—LUKE xvii. 21

I will be glad, and rejoice in Thy mercy: for Thou hast considered my trouble; Thou hast known my soul in adversities.

—PSALM xxxi. 7

God knows us through and through. Not the most secret thought, which we most hide from ourselves, is hidden from Him. As then we come to know ourselves through and through, we come to see ourselves more as God sees us, and then we catch some little glimpse of His designs with us, how each ordering of His Providence, each check to our desires, each failure of our hopes, is just fitted for us, and for something in our own spiritual state, which others know not of, and which, till then, we knew not. Until we come to this knowledge, we must take all in faith, believing, though we know not, the goodness of God towards us. As we know ourselves, we, thus far, know God.

EDWARD BOUVERIE PUSEY

We know that all things work together for good to them that love God.

—ROMANS viii. 28

He does not need to transplant us into a different field, but right where we are, with just the circumstances that surround us, He makes His sun to shine and His dew to fall upon us, and transforms the very things that were before our greatest hindrances, into the chiefest and most blessed means of our growth.

HANNAH WHITALL SMITH

I will both lay me down in peace, and sleep: for Thou, Lord, only makest me dwell in safety.

—PSALM iv. 8

We sleep in peace in the arms of God, when we yield ourselves up to His providence, in a delightful consciousness of His tender mercies; no more restless uncertainties, no more anxious desires, no more impatience at the place we are in; for it is God who has put us there, and who holds us in His arms. Can we be unsafe where He has placed us?

FRANÇOIS DE LA MOTHE FÉNELON

In all thy ways acknowledge Him, and He shall direct thy paths.

—PROVERBS iii. 6

One evening when Luther saw a little bird perched on a tree, to roost there for the night, he said, "This little bird has had its supper, and now it is getting ready to go to sleep here, quite secure and content, never troubling itself what its food will be, or where its lodging on the morrow. Like David, it 'abides under the shadow of the Almighty.' It sits on its little twig content, and lets God take care."

MARTIN LUTHER

Your heavenly Father knoweth that ye have need of all these things.

—MATTHEW vi. 32

THAT spirit which suffices quiet hearts, which seems to come forth to such from every dry knoll of sere grass, from every pinestump, and half-embedded stone, on which the dull March sun shines, comes forth to the poor and hungry, and to such as are of simple taste. If thou fill thy brain with Boston and New York, with fashion and covetousness, and wilt stimulate thy jaded senses with wine and French coffee, thou shalt find no radiance of wisdom in the lonely waste of the pine-woods.

RALPH WALDO EMERSON

14

As for me, I will behold Thy face in righteousness;
I shall be satisfied, when I awake, with Thy
likeness.

—PSALM xvii. 15

*A*s a countenance is made beautiful by
the soul's shining through it, so the
world is beautiful by the shining
through it of a God.

FRIEDRICH   HEINRICH   JACOBI

15

The eternal God is thy refuge, and underneath are the everlasting arms.

—DEUTERONOMY xxxiii. 27

"T he Everlasting Arms." I think of that whenever rest is sweet. How the whole earth and the strength of it, that is almightiness, is beneath every tired creature to give it rest; *holding* us, always! No thought of God is closer than that. No human tenderness of patience is greater than that which gathers in its arms a little child, and holds it, heedless of weariness. And He fills the great earth, and all upon it, with this unseen force of His love, that never forgets or exhausts itself, so that everywhere we may lie down in His bosom, and be comforted.

ADELINE D. T. WHITNEY

Show me Thy ways, O Lord; teach me Thy paths.

—PSALM xxv. 4

Go on in all simplicity; do not be so anxious to win a quiet mind, and it will be all the quieter. Do not examine so closely into the progress of your soul. Do not crave so much to be perfect, but let your spiritual life be formed by your duties, and by the actions which are called forth by circumstances. Do not take overmuch thought for to-morrow. God, who has led you safely on so far, will lead you on to the end. Be altogether at rest in the loving holy confidence which you ought to have in His heavenly Providence.

SAINT FRANCIS DE SALES

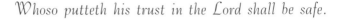

Whoso putteth his trust in the Lord shall be safe.

—PROVERBS xxix. 25

*I*n the darkest hour through which a human soul can pass, whatever else is doubtful, this at least is certain. If there be no God and no future state, yet even then, it is better to be generous than selfish, better to be chaste than licentious, better to be true than false, better to be brave than to be a coward. Blessed beyond all earthly blessedness is the man who, in the tempestuous darkness of the soul, has dared to hold fast to these venerable landmarks. Thrice blessed is he, who, when all is drear and cheerless within and without, when his teachers terrify him, and his friends shrink from him, has obstinately clung to moral good. Thrice blessed, because *his* night shall pass into clear, bright day.

FREDERICK WILLIAM ROBERTSON

Behold, I am with thee, and will keep thee in all places whither thou goest.

—GENESIS xxviii. 15

We must leave to God all that depends on Him, and think only of being faithful in all that depends upon ourselves. When God takes away that which He has given you, He knows well how to replace it, either through other means or by Himself.

FRANÇOIS DE LA MOTHE FÉNELON

I sought the Lord, and He heard me, and delivered me from all my fears.

—PSALM xxxiv. 4

TAKE courage, and turn your troubles, which are without remedy, into material for spiritual progress. Often turn to our Lord, who is watching you, poor frail little being as you are, amid your labors and distractions. He sends you help, and blesses your affliction. This thought should enable you to bear your troubles patiently and gently, for love of Him who only allows you to be tried for your own good. Raise your heart continually to God, seek His aid, and let the foundation stone of your consolation be your happiness in being His. All vexations and annoyances will be comparatively unimportant while you know that you have such a Friend, such a Stay, such a Refuge. May God be ever in your heart.

SAINT FRANCIS DE SALES

I will bless the Lord, who hath given me counsel.

—PSALM xvi. 7

O Truth who art Eternity!
And Love who art Truth!
And Eternity who art Love!
Thou art my God, to Thee do I
sigh night and day. When I first
knew Thee, Thou liftedst me
up, that I might see there was
somewhat for me to see, and that I
was not yet such as to see. And Thou
streaming forth Thy beams of light
upon me most strongly, didst beat back
the weakness of my sight, and I trembled
with love and awe: and I perceived myself to
be far off from Thee in the region of unlikeness.

SAINT AUGUSTINE

Wait on the Lord: be of good courage, and He shall strengthen thine heart: wait, I say, on the Lord.

*A*s soon as we are with God in faith and in love, we are in prayer.

FRANÇOIS DE LA MOTHE FÉNELON

❧

*W*e need only obey. There is guidance for each of us, and by lowly listening we shall hear the right word.

RALPH WALDO EMERSON

Let the heart of them rejoice that seek the Lord.

—PSALM cv. 3

I do not know when I have had happier times in my soul, than when I have been sitting at work, with nothing before me but a candle and a white cloth, and hearing no sound but that of my own breath, with God in my soul and heaven in my eye. . . . I rejoice in being exactly what I am,— a creature capable of loving God, and who, as long as God lives, must be happy. I get up and look for a while out of the window, and gaze at the moon and stars, the work of an Almighty hand. I think of the grandeur of the universe, and then sit down, and think myself one of the happiest beings in it.

ANONYMOUS

And I have also given thee that which thou hast not asked.

—1 Kings iii. 13

*T*he highest pinnacle of the spiritual life is not happy joy in unbroken sunshine, but absolute and undoubting trust in the love of God.

Anthony Wilson Thorold

24

Bear ye one another's burdens, and so fulfil the law of Christ.

—GALATIANS vi. 2

However perplexed you may at any hour become about some question of truth, one refuge and resource is always at hand: you can do something for some one besides yourself. When your own burden is heaviest, you can always lighten a little some other burden. At the times when you cannot see God, there is still open to you this sacred possibility, to *show* God; for it is the love and kindness of human hearts through which the divine reality comes home to men, whether they name it or not. Let this thought, then, stay with you: there may be times when you cannot find help, but there is no time when you cannot give help.

GEORGE S. MERRIAM

25

He healeth the broken in heart, and bindeth up their wounds. He telleth the number of the stars; He calleth them all by their names.

—PSALM cxlvii. 3–4

I looked up to the heavens once more, and the quietness of the stars seemed to reproach me. "We are safe up here," they seemed to say; "we shine, fearless and confident, for the God who gave the primrose its rough leaves to hide it from the blast of uneven spring, hangs us in the awful hollows of space. We cannot fall out of His safety. Lift up your eyes on high, and behold! Who hath created these things—that bringeth out their host by number? He calleth them all by names. By the greatness of His might, for that He is strong in power, not one faileth. Why sayest thou, O Jacob! and speakest, O Israel! my way is hid from the Lord, and my judgment is passed over from my God?"

GEORGE MACDONALD

Because Thy loving-kindness is better than life, my lips shall praise Thee.

—PSALM lxiii. 3

A root set in the finest soil, in the best climate, and blessed with all that sun and air and rain can do for it, is not in so sure a way of its growth to perfection, as every man may be, whose spirit aspires after all that which God is ready and infinitely desirous to give him. For the sun meets not the springing bud that stretches towards him with half that certainty, as God, the source of all good, communicates Himself to the soul that longs to partake of Him.

WILLIAM LAW

27

Rejoice evermore. . . . In everything give thanks.

—1 THESSALONIANS v. 16, 18

Gratitude consists in a watchful, minute attention to the particulars of our state, and to the multitude of God's gifts, taken one by one. It fills us with a consciousness that God loves and cares for us, even to the least event and the smallest need of life. It is a blessed thought, that from our childhood God has been laying His fatherly hands upon us, and always in benediction; that even the strokes of His hands are blessings, and among the chiefest we have ever received. When this feeling is awakened, the heart beats with a pulse of thankfulness. Every gift has its return of praise. It awakens an unceasing daily converse with our Father,—He speaking to us by the descent of blessings, we to Him by the ascent of thanksgiving. And all our whole life is thereby drawn under the light of His countenance, and is filled with a gladness, serenity, and peace.

HENRY EDWARD MANNING

I will praise Thee, O Lord, with my whole heart; I will show forth all Thy marvellous works.

—PSALM ix. 1

I have experienced that the habit of taking out of the hand of our Lord every little blessing and brightness on our path, confirms us, in an especial manner, in communion with His love.

MARY ANNE SCHIMMELPENNINCK

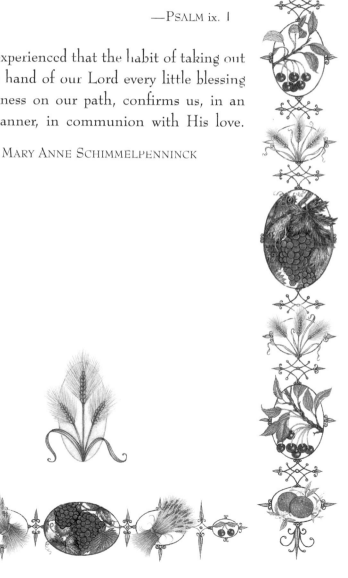

Beloved, let us love one another: for love is of God; and every one that loveth is born of God, and knoweth God.

—1 JOHN iv. 7

The Spirit of Love, wherever it is, is its own blessing and happiness, because it is the truth and reality of God in the soul; and therefore is in the same joy of life, and is the same good to itself everywhere and on every occasion. Would you know the blessing of all blessings? It is this God of Love dwelling in your soul, and killing every root of bitterness, which is the pain and torment of every earthly, selfish love. For all wants are satisfied, all disorders of nature are removed, no life is any longer a burden, every day is a day of peace, everything you meet becomes a help to you, because everything you see or do is all done in the sweet, gentle element of Love.

WILLIAM LAW

Trust in the Lord, and do good; so shalt thou dwell in the land, and verily thou shalt be fed.

—PSALM xxxvii. 3

*C*onsider that all which appears beautiful outwardly, is solely derived from the invisible Spirit which is the source of that external beauty, and say joyfully, "Behold these are streamlets from the uncreated Fountain; behold, these are drops from the infinite Ocean of all good! Oh! how does my inmost heart rejoice at the thought of that eternal, infinite Beauty, which is the source and origin of all created beauty!"

LORENZO SCUPOLI

Thou shalt be stedfast, and shalt not fear: because thou shalt forget thy misery, and remember it as waters that pass away.

—JOB xi. 15–16

God has brought us into this time; He, and not ourselves or some dark demon. If we are not fit to cope with that which He has prepared for us, we should have been utterly unfit for any condition that we imagine for ourselves. In this time we are to live and wrestle, and in no other. Let us humbly, tremblingly, manfully look at it, and we shall not wish that the sun could go back its ten degrees, or that we could go back with it. If easy times are departed, it is that the difficult times may make us more in earnest; that they may teach us not to depend upon ourselves. If easy belief is impossible, it is that we may learn what belief is, and in whom it is to be placed.

FREDERICK DENISON MAURICE

I will cry unto God most high; unto God, that performeth all things for me.

—PSALM lvii. 2

*I*t is faith's work to claim and challenge loving-kindness out of all the roughest strokes of God.

SAMUEL RUTHERFORD

I praise Thee while my days go on;
I love Thee while my days go on:
Through dark and dearth, through fire and frost,
With emptied arms and treasure lost,
I thank Thee while my days go on.

ELIZABETH BARRETT BROWNING

33

Nor trust in uncertain riches, but in the living God, who giveth us richly all things to enjoy.

—1 TIMOTHY vi. 17

Be of good faith, my dear Friends, look not out at any thing; fear none of those things ye may be exposed to suffer, either outwardly or inwardly; but trust the Lord over all, and your life will spring, and grow, and refresh you, and ye will learn obedience and faithfulness daily more and more, even by your exercises and sufferings; yea, the Lord will teach you the very mystery of faith and obedience; the wisdom, power, love, and goodness of the Lord ordering *every* thing for you, and ordering *your* hearts in every thing.

ISAAC PENINGTON

34

Delight thyself also in the Lord; and He shall give thee the desires of thine heart.

—PSALM xxxvii. 4

All who call on God in true faith, earnestly from the heart, will certainly be heard, and will receive what they have asked and desired, although not in the hour or in the measure, or the very thing which they ask; yet, they will obtain something greater and more glorious than they had dared to ask.

MARTIN LUTHER

35

The temple of God is holy, which temple ye are.

—1 CORINTHIANS iii. 17

*T*his pearl of eternity is the church or temple of God within thee, the consecrated place of divine worship, where alone thou canst worship God in spirit and in truth. When once thou art well grounded in this inward worship, thou wilt have learned to live unto God above time and place. For every day will be Sunday to thee, and, wherever thou goest, thou wilt have a priest, a church, and an altar along with thee. For when God has all that He should have of thy heart, when thou art wholly given up to the obedience of the light and spirit of God within thee, to will only in His will, to love only in His love, to be wise only in His wisdom, then it is that everything thou doest is as a song of praise, and the common business of thy life is a conforming to God's will on earth as angels do in heaven.

WILLIAM LAW

36

Thou shalt guide me with Thy counsel, and afterward receive me to glory.

—PSALM lxxiii. 24

*I*f we stand in the openings of the present moment, with all the length and breadth of our faculties unselfishly adjusted to what it reveals, we are in the best condition to receive what God is always ready to communicate.

THOMAS COGSWELL UPHAM

I will lift up mine eyes unto the hills, from whence cometh my help.

My help cometh from the Lord, which made heaven and earth.

He will not suffer thy foot to be moved; He that keepeth thee will not slumber.

Behold, He that keepeth Israel shall neither slumber nor sleep.

The Lord is thy keeper: the Lord is thy shade upon thy right hand.

The sun shall not smite thee by day, nor the moon by night.

The Lord shall preserve thee from all evil: He shall preserve thy soul.

The Lord shall preserve thy going out and thy coming in from this time forth, and even for evermore.

—PSALM cxxi

SUPPORT

If we walk in the light, as He is in the light, we will have fellowship one with another.

—1 JOHN i. 7

Thou wilt keep him in perfect peace, whose mind is stayed on Thee: because he trusteth in Thee.

—ISAIAH xxvi. 3

God is a tranquil Being, and abides in a tranquil eternity. So must thy spirit become a tranquil and clear little pool, wherein the serene light of God can be mirrored. Therefore shun all that is disquieting and distracting, both within and without. Nothing in the whole world is worth the loss of thy peace; even the faults which thou has committed should only humble, but not disquiet thee. God is full of joy, peace, and happiness. Endeavor then to obtain a continually joyful and peaceful spirit. Avoid all anxious care, vexation, murmuring, and melancholy, which darken thy soul, and render thee unfit for the friendship of God. If thou dost perceive such feelings arising, turn gently away from them.

GERHARD TERSTEEGEN

That which I see not, teach Thou me.

—JOB xxxiv. 32

*T*each me your mood, O patient stars!
    Who climb each night the ancient sky
Leaving on space no shade, no scars,
    No trace of age, no fear to die.

RALPH WALDO EMERSON

See that ye refuse not Him that speaketh.

—HEBREWS xii. 25

There is hardly ever a complete silence in our soul. God is whispering to us wellnigh incessantly. Whenever the sounds of the world die out in the soul, or sink low, then we hear these whisperings of God. He is always whispering to us, only we do not always hear, because of the noise, hurry, and distraction which life causes as it rushes on.

FREDERICK WILLIAM FABER

The Lord is my light and my salvation; whom shall I fear? The Lord is the strength of my life; of whom shall I be afraid?

—PSALM xxvii. 1

When therefore the smallest instinct or desire of thy heart calleth thee towards God, and a newness of life, give it time and leave to speak; and take care thou refuse not Him that speaketh. Be retired, silent, passive, and humbly attentive to this new risen light within thee.

WILLIAM LAW

*In the multitude of my thoughts within me Thy
comforts delight my soul.*

—PSALM xciv. 19

*L*et every creature have your love. Love, with
its fruits of meekness, patience, and humility, is all that we can wish for to ourselves, and our
fellow-creatures; for this is to live in God, united
to Him, both for time and eternity. To desire to
communicate good to every creature, in the degree
we can, and it is capable of receiving from us, is a
divine temper; for thus God stands unchangeably
disposed towards the whole creation.

WILLIAM LAW

My little children, let us not love in word, neither in tongue; but in deed, and in truth.

—1 JOHN iii. 18

What shall be our reward for loving our neighbor *as* ourselves in this life? That, when we become angels, we shall be enabled to love him *better* than ourselves.

EMANUEL SWEDENBORG

Blessed are the peacemakers: for they shall be called the children of God.

—MATTHEW v. 9

People are always expecting to get peace in heaven; but you know whatever peace they get there will be ready-made. Whatever making of peace *they* can be blest for, must be on the earth here: not the taking of arms against, but the building of nests amidst, its sea of troubles like the halcyons. Difficult enough, you think? Perhaps so, but I do not see that any of us try. We complain of the want of many things—we want votes, we want liberty, we want amusement, we want money. Which of us feels or knows that he wants peace?

JOHN RUSKIN

I beseech you therefore, brethren, by the mercies of God, that ye present your bodies a living sacrifice, holy, acceptable unto God, which is your reasonable service.

—ROMANS xii. 1

May it not be a comfort to those of us who feel we have not the mental or spiritual power that others have, to notice that the living sacrifice mentioned in Romans is our "bodies"?

Of course, that includes the mental power, but does it not also include the loving, sympathizing glance, the kind, encouraging word, *the ready errand for another*, the work of our hands, opportunities for all of which come oftener in the day than for the mental power we are often tempted to envy? May we be enabled to offer willingly that which we have.

ANONYMOUS

47

Let all those that put their trust in Thee rejoice: . . . let them also that love Thy name be joyful in Thee.

—PSALM v. 11

What inexpressible joy for me, to look up through the apple-blossoms and the fluttering leaves, and to see God's love there; to listen to the thrush that has built his nest among them, and to feel God's love, who cares for the birds, in every note that swells his little throat; to look beyond to the bright blue depths of the sky, and to feel they are a canopy of blessing,—the roof of the house of my Father; that if the clouds pass over it, it is the unchangeable light they veil; that, even when the day itself passes, I shall see that the night itself only unveils new worlds of light; and to know that if I could unwrap fold after fold of God's universe, I should only unfold more and more blessing, and see deeper and deeper into the love which is at the heart of all.

ELIZABETH CHARLES

The fruit of the Spirit is love, joy, peace, long-suffering, gentleness, goodness, faith, meekness, temperance.

—GALATIANS v. 22, 23

*T*he universe appears before my eyes under a transformed aspect. The dead, heavy mass which did but stop up space has vanished, and in its place there flows onward, with the rushing music of mighty waves an eternal stream of life, and power, and action, which issues from the original source of all life,—from Thy life, O Infinite One! for all life is Thy life, and only the religious eye penetrates to the realm of true Beauty.

JOHANN GOTTLIEB FICHTE

Thou hast made him exceeding glad with Thy countenance.

—PSALM xxi. 6

A new day rose upon me. It was as if another sun had risen into the sky; the heavens were indescribably brighter, and the earth fairer; and that day has gone on brightening to the present hour. I have known the other joys of life, I suppose, as much as most men; I have known art and beauty, music and gladness; I have known friendship and love and family ties; but it is certain that till we see GOD in the world—GOD in the bright and boundless universe—we never know the highest joy. It is far more than if one were translated to a world a thousand times fairer than this; for that supreme and central Light of Infinite Love and Wisdom, shining over this world and all worlds, alone can show us how noble and beautiful, how fair and glorious they are.

ORVILLE DEWEY

Giving thanks always for all things unto God.

—EPHESIANS v. 20

When I look like this into the blue sky, it seems so deep, so peaceful, so full of a mysterious tenderness, that I could lie for centuries and wait for the dawning of the face of God out of the awful loving-kindness.

GEORGE MACDONALD

For He satisfieth the longing soul, and filleth the hungry soul with goodness.

—PSALM cvii. 9

He showed a little thing, the quantity of a hazel-nut, lying in the palm of my hand, and it was as round as a ball. I looked thereon with the eye of my understanding, and thought, *"What may this be?"* and it was answered generally thus, *"It is all that is made."* I marvelled how it might last; for methought it might suddenly have fallen to naught for littleness. And I was answered in my understanding, *"It lasteth, and ever shall: For God loveth it. And so hath all things being by Love of God."*

MOTHER JULIANA

52

For the whole world before Thee is as a little grain of the balance, yea, as a drop of the morning dew that falleth down upon the earth. But Thou hast mercy upon all. For Thou lovest all the things that are.

—WISDOM OF SOLOMON xi. 22–24

God makes every common thing serve, if thou wilt, to enlarge that capacity of bliss in His love. Not a prayer, not an act of faithfulness in your calling, not a self-denying or kind word or deed, done out of love for Himself; not a weariness or painfulness endured patiently; not a duty performed; not a temptation resisted; but it enlarges the whole soul for the endless capacity of the love of God.

EDWARD BOUVERIE PUSEY

If we love one another, God dwelleth in us, and His love is perfected in us.

—1 JOHN iv. 12

Certainly, in our own little sphere it is not the most active people to whom we owe the most. Among the common people whom we know, it is not necessarily those who are busiest, not those who, meteor-like, are ever on the rush after some visible charge and work. It is the lives, like the stars, which simply pour down on us the calm light of their bright and faithful being, up to which we look and out of which we gather the deepest calm and courage. It seems to me that there is reassurance here for many of us who seem to have no chance for active usefulness. We can do nothing for our fellow-men. But still it is good to know that we can be something for them; to know (and this we may know surely) that no man or woman of the humblest sort can really be strong, gentle, pure, and good, without the world being better for it, without somebody being helped and comforted by the very existence of that goodness.

PHILLIPS BROOKS

Are they not all ministering spirits?

—HEBREWS i. 14

M ay I reach
That purest heaven, be to other souls
The cup of strength in some great agony,
Enkindle generous ardor, feed pure love,
Be the sweet presence of a good diffused,
And in diffusion ever more intense!
So shall I join the choir invisible
Whose music is the gladness of the world.

GEORGE ELIOT

Consider the lilies of the field, how they grow.

—MATTHEW vi. 28

*T*HINE own self-will and anxiety, thy hurry and labor, disturb thy peace, and prevent Me from working in thee. Look at the little flowers, in the serene summer days; they quietly open their petals, and the sun shines into them with his gentle influences. So will I do for thee, if thou wilt yield thyself to Me.

GERHARD TERSTEEGEN

56

The Lord bless thee, and keep thee: the Lord make His face shine upon thee, and be gracious unto thee: the Lord lift up His countenance upon thee, and give thee peace.

—NUMBERS vi. 24–26

GOD so loveth us that He would make all things channels to us and messengers of His love. Do for His sake deeds of love, and He will give thee His love. Still thyself, thy own cares, thy own thoughts for Him, and He will speak to thy heart. Ask for Himself, and He will give thee Himself. Truly, a secret hidden thing is the love of God, known only to them who seek it, and to them also secret, for what man can have of it here is how slight a foretaste of that endless ocean of His love!

EDWARD BOUVERIE PUSEY

The Lord my God will enlighten my darkness.

—PSALM xviii. 28

We listened to a man whom we felt to be, with all his heart and soul and strength, striving against whatever was mean and unmanly and unrighteous in our little world. It was not the cold clear voice of one giving advice and warning from serene heights to those who were struggling and sinning below, but the warm living voice of one who was fighting for us and by our sides, and calling on us to help him and ourselves and one another. And so, wearily and little by little, but surely and steadily on the whole, was brought home to the young boy, for the first time, the meaning of his life; that it was no fool's or sluggard's paradise into which he had wandered by chance, but a battle-field ordained from of old, where there are no spectators, but the youngest must take his side, and the stakes are life and death.

THOMAS HUGHES

As he thinketh in his heart, so is he.

—PROVERBS xxiii. 7

Still may Thy sweet mercy spread
A shady arm above my head,
About my paths; so shall I find
The fair centre of my mind
Thy temple, and those lovely walls
Bright ever with a beam that falls
Fresh from the pure glance of Thine eye,
Lighting to eternity.

RICHARD CRASHAW

He that loveth not knoweth not God; for God is love.

—1 John iv. 8

Into all our lives, in many simple, familiar, homely ways, God infuses this element of joy from the surprises of life, which unexpectedly brighten our days, and fill our eyes with light. He drops this added sweetness into His children's cup, and makes it to run over. The success we were not counting on, the blessing we were not trying after, the strain of music, in the midst of drudgery, the beautiful morning picture or sunset glory thrown in as we pass to or from our daily business, the unsought word of encouragement or expression of sympathy, the sentence that meant for us more than the writer or speaker thought,—these and a hundred others that every one's experience can supply are instances of what I mean. You may call it accident or chance—it often is; you may call it human goodness—it often is; but always, always call it God's love, for that is always in it.

Samuel Longfellow

To be spiritually minded is life and peace.

—ROMANS viii. 6

S erene will be our days and bright,
   And happy will our nature be,
When love is an unerring light,
   And joy its own security.

WILLIAM WORDSWORTH

L et us always remember that holiness does
   not consist in doing uncommon things,
but in doing everything with purity of heart.

HENRY EDWARD MANNING

He that abideth in Me, and I in him, bringeth forth much fruit.

—JOHN xv. 5

*N*othing less than the majesty of God, and the powers of the world to come, can maintain the peace and sanctity of our homes, the order and serenity of our minds, the spirit of patience and tender mercy in our hearts. Then will even the merest drudgery of duty cease to humble us, when we transfigure it by the glory of our own spirit.

JAMES MARTINEAU

62

The Lord is my strength, and my shield; my heart trusted in Him, and I am helped: therefore my heart greatly rejoiceth; and with my song will I praise Him.

—PSALM xxviii. 7

*M*ake yourselves nests of pleasant thoughts. None of us yet know, for none of us have been taught in early youth, what fairy palaces we may build of beautiful thought— proof against all adversity. Bright fancies, satisfied memories, noble histories, faithful sayings, treasure-houses of precious and restful thoughts, which care cannot disturb, nor pain make gloomy, nor poverty take away from us,—houses built without hands, for our souls to live in.

JOHN RUSKIN

63

If I take the wings of the morning, and dwell in the uttermost parts of the sea: even there shall Thy hand lead me, and Thy right hand shall hold me.

—PSALM cxxxix. 9–10

*H*ow can we come to perceive this direct leading of God? By a careful looking at home, and abiding within the gates of thy own soul. Therefore, let a man be at home in his own heart, and cease from his restless chase of and search after outward things. If he is thus at home while on earth, he will surely come to see what there is to be done at home,—what God commands him inwardly without means, and also outwardly by the help of means; and then let him surrender himself, and follow God along whatever path his loving Lord thinks fit to lead him: whether it be to contemplation or action, to usefulness or enjoyment; whether in sorrow or in joy, let him follow on.

JOHN TAULER

64

If thou canst believe, all things are possible to him that believeth.

—MARK ix. 23

We have only to be patient, to pray, and to do His will, according to our present light and strength, and the growth of the soul will go on. The plant grows in the mist and under clouds as truly as under sunshine. So does the heavenly principle within.

WILLIAM ELLERY CHANNING

If we hope for that we see not, then do we with patience wait for it.

—ROMANS viii. 25

I believe that if we could only see beforehand what it is that our heavenly Father means us to be,—the *soul* beauty and perfection and glory, the glorious and lovely spiritual body that this soul is to dwell in through all eternity,—if we could have a glimpse of *this*, we should not grudge all the trouble and pains He is taking with us now, to bring us up to that ideal, which is His thought of us. We know that it is God's way to work slowly, so we must not be surprised if He takes a great many years of discipline to turn a mortal being into an immortal, glorious angel.

ANNIE KEARY

Well done, good and faithful servant; thou hast been faithful over a few things, I will make thee ruler over many things: enter thou into the joy of thy Lord.

—MATTHEW xxv. 23

My mind is forever closed against embarrassment and perplexity, against uncertainty, doubt, and anxiety; my heart against grief and desire. Calm and unmoved, I look down on all things, for I know that I cannot explain a single event, nor comprehend its connection with that which alone concerns me. In His world all things prosper; this satisfies me, and in this belief I stand fast as a rock. My breast is steeled against annoyance on account of personal offences and vexations, or exultation in personal merit; for my whole personality has disappeared in the contemplation of the purpose of my being.

JOHANN GOTTLIEB FICHTE

67

The Lord is my shepherd; I shall not want.

He maketh me to lie down in green pastures: He leadeth me beside the still waters.

He restoreth my soul: He leadeth me in the paths of righteousness for His name's sake.

Yea, though I walk through the valley of the shadow of death, I will fear no evil; for Thou art with me; Thy rod and Thy staff they comfort me.

Thou preparest a table before me in the presence of mine enemies: Thou anointest my head with oil; my cup runneth over.

Surely goodness and mercy shall follow me all the days of my life: and I will dwell in the house of the Lord for ever.

—PSALM xxiii

FORTITUDE

Strengthened with all might, according to His glorious power, unto all patience and longsuffering with joyousness.

—COLOSSIANS i. 11

Be strong and of a good courage; be not afraid,
neither be thou dismayed: for the Lord thy God
is with thee whithersoever thou goest.

—JOSHUA i. 9

Watch your way then, as a
cautious traveller; and don't
be gazing at that mountain or
river in the distance, and saying,
"How shall I ever get over them?"
but keep to the present *little inch* that
is before you, and accomplish *that* in
the little moment that belongs to it.
The mountain and the river can
only be passed in the same way;
and, when you come to them, you
will come to the light and strength
that belong to them.

MARY ANN KELTY

70

The shadow of a great rock in a weary land.

—ISAIAH xxxii. 2

Be like the promontory, against which the waves continually break; but it stands firm, and tames the fury of the water around it. Unhappy am I, because this has happened to me? Not so, but happy am I, though this has happened to me, because I continue free from pain, neither crushed by the present, nor fearing the future. Will then this which has happened prevent thee from being just, magnanimous, temperate, prudent, secure against inconsiderate opinions and falsehood? Remember, too, on every occasion which leads thee to vexation to apply this principle: that this is not a misfortune, but that to bear it nobly is good fortune.

MARCUS AURELIUS ANTONINUS

71

My brethren, count it all joy when ye fall into divers temptations; knowing this, that the trying of your faith worketh patience.

—James i. 2–3

We have need of patience with ourselves and with others; with those below, and those above us, and with our own equals; with those who love us and those who love us not; for the greatest things and for the least; against sudden inroads of trouble, and under daily burdens; disappointments as to the weather, or the breaking of the heart; in the weariness of the body, or the wearing of the soul; in our own failure of duty, or others' failure toward us; in every-day wants, or in the aching of sickness or the decay of old age; in disappointment, bereavement, losses, injuries, reproaches; in heaviness of the heart; or its sickness amid delayed hopes. In all these things, from childhood's little troubles to the martyr's sufferings, patience is the grace of God, whereby we endure evil for the love of God.

Edward Bouverie Pusey

That ye might be filled with all the fulness of God.

—Ephesians iii.19

O GOD, the Life of the faithful, the Bliss of the righteous, mercifully receive the prayers of Thy suppliants, that the souls which thirst for Thy promises may evermore be filled from Thy abundance. Amen.

Gelasian Sacramentary

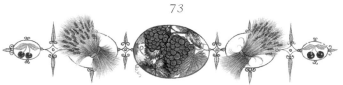

The hand of our God is upon all of them for good that seek Him.

—EZRA viii. 22

*I*t is not by seeking more fertile regions where toil is lighter—happier circumstances free from difficult complications and troublesome people—but by bringing the high courage of a devout soul, clear in principle and aim, to bear upon what is given to us, that we brighten our inward light, lead something of a true life, and introduce the kingdom of heaven into the midst of our earthly day. If we cannot work out the will of God where God has placed us, then why has He placed us there?

JOHN HAMILTON THOM

He giveth power to the faint; and to them that have no might He increaseth strength.

—ISAIAH xl. 29

S hould we feel at times disheartened and discouraged, a confiding thought, a simple movement of heart towards God will renew our powers. Whatever He may demand of us, He will give us at the moment the strength and the courage that we need.

FRANÇOIS DE LA MOTHE FÉNELON

The Lord is good to all: and His tender mercies are over all His works.

—PSALM cxlv. 9

We are ready to praise when all shines fair; but when life is overcast, when all things seem to be against us, when we are in fear for some cherished happiness, or in the depths of sorrow, or in the solitude of a life which has no visible support, or in a season of sickness, and with the shadow of death approaching,—then to praise God; then to say, This fear, loneliness, affliction, pain, and trembling awe are as sure tokens of love, as life, health, joy, and the gifts of home.

HENRY EDWARD MANNING

As we have therefore opportunity, let us do good unto all men.

—GALATIANS vi. 10

Oh, when we turn away from some duty or some fellow-creature, saying that our hearts are too sick and sore with some great yearning of our own, we may often sever the line on which a divine message was coming to us. We shut out the man, and we shut out the angel who had sent him on to open the door. There is a plan working in our lives; and if we keep our hearts quiet and our eyes open, it all works together; and, if we don't, it all fights together, and goes on fighting till it comes right, somehow, somewhere.

ANNIE KEARY

I the Lord will hold thy right hand, saying unto thee,
fear not; I will help thee.

—ISAIAH xli. 13

*D*o not look forward to the changes and chances of this life in fear; rather look to them with full hope that, as they arise, God, whose you are, will deliver you out of them. He has kept you hitherto,—do you but hold fast to His dear Hand, and He will lead you safely through all things; and, when you cannot stand, He will bear you in His arms. Do not look forward to what may happen to-morrow; the same everlasting Father who cares for you to-day, will take care of you to-morrow, and every day. Either He will shield you from suffering, or He will give you unfailing strength to bear it. Be at peace then, and put aside all anxious thoughts and imaginations.

SAINT FRANCIS DE SALES

78

Pray for us unto the Lord thy God . . . that the Lord thy God may show us the way wherein we may walk, and the thing that we may do.

—JEREMIAH xlii. 2–3

We can't choose happiness either for ourselves or for another; we can't tell where that will lie. We can only choose whether we will indulge ourselves in the present moment, or whether we will renounce that, for the sake of obeying the Divine voice within us,—for the sake of being true to all the motives that sanctify our lives. I know this belief is hard; it has slipped away from me again and again; but I have felt that if I let it go forever, I should have no light through the darkness of this life.

GEORGE ELIOT

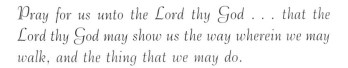

Let not your heart be troubled, neither let it be afraid.

—JOHN xiv. 27

Be not afraid of those trials which God may see fit to send upon thee. It is with the wind and storm of tribulation that God separates the true wheat from the chaff. Always remember, therefore, that God comes to thee in thy sorrows, as really as in thy joys. He lays low, and He builds up. Thou wilt find thyself far from perfection, if thou dost not find God in everything.

MIGUEL DE MOLINOS

In the day when I cried Thou answeredst me, and strengthenedst me with strength in my soul.

—PSALM cxxxviii. 3

*C*ast thy burdens upon the Lord,—hand it over, heave it upon Him, *and He shall sustain thee;* shall bear both, if thou trust Him with both, both thee and thy burden. *He shall never suffer the righteous to be moved.*

ROBERT LEIGHTON

I sought the Lord, and He heard me, and delivered me from all my fears.

—PSALM xxxiv. 4

God beholds thee individually, whoever thou art. "He calls thee by thy name." He sees thee, and understands thee.

He knows what is in thee, all thy own peculiar feelings and thoughts, thy dispositions and likings, thy strength and thy weakness.

He views thee in thy day of rejoicing and thy day of sorrow.

He sympathizes in thy hopes and in thy temptations; He interests himself in all thy anxieties and thy remembrances, in all the risings and fallings of thy spirit.

He compasses thee round, and bears thee in His arms; He takes thee up and sets thee down.

Thou dost not love thyself better than He loves thee. Thou canst not shrink from pain more than he dislikes thy bearing it, and if He puts it on thee, it is as thou wilt put it on thyself, if thou art wise, for a greater good afterwards.

JOHN HENRY NEWMAN

Your Father knoweth what things ye have need of.

—MATTHEW vi. 8

*I*t has been well said that no man ever sank under the burden of the day. It is when to-morrow's burden is added to the burden of to-day that the weight is more than a man can bear. Never load yourselves so, my friends. If you find yourselves so loaded, at least remember this: it is your own doing, not God's. He begs you to leave the future to Him, and mind the present.

GEORGE MACDONALD

Love is of God; and every one that loveth is born of God, and knoweth God.

—1 JOHN iv. 7

There is a faith in God, and a clear perception of His will and designs, and providence, and glory, which gives to its possessor a confidence and patience and sweet composure, under every varied and troubling aspect of events, such as no man can realize who has not felt its influences in his own heart. There is a communion with God, in which the soul feels the presence of the unseen One, in the profound depths of its being, with a vivid distinctness and a holy reverence, such as no words can describe. There is a state of union with God, I do not say often reached, yet it has been attained in this world, in which all the past and present and future seem reconciled, and eternity is won and enjoyed; and God and man, earth and heaven, with all their mysteries, are apprehended in truth as they lie in the mind of the Infinite.

SAMUEL DOWSE ROBBINS

And the Lord make you to increase and abound in love, one toward another, and toward all men.

—1 THESSALONIANS iii. 12

Some say that the age of chivalry is past. The age of chivalry is never past, so long as there is a wrong left unredressed on earth, or a man or woman left to say, "I will redress that wrong, or spend my life in the attempt." The age of chivalry is never past, so long as we have faith enough to say, "God will help me to redress that wrong; or, if not me, He will help those that come after me, for His eternal Will is to overcome evil with good."

CHARLES KINGSLEY

Therefore, my beloved brethren, be ye stedfast, unmoveable, always abounding in the work of the Lord, forasmuch as ye know that your labor is not in vain in the Lord.

—1 CORINTHIANS xv. 58

Did you ever hear of a man who had striven all his life faithfully and singly toward an object and in no measure obtained it? If a man constantly aspires, is he not elevated? Did ever a man try heroism, magnanimity, truth, sincerity and find that there was no advantage in them,—that it was a vain endeavor?

HENRY DAVID THOREAU

His delight is in the law of the Lord. . . . And he shall be like a tree planted by the rivers of water, that bringeth forth his fruit in his season; his leaf also shall not wither; and whatsoever he doeth shall prosper.

—PSALM i. 2–3

*T*o shape the whole Future is not our problem; but only to shape faithfully a small part of it, according to rules already known. It is perhaps possible for each of us, who will with due earnestness inquire, to ascertain clearly what he, for his own part, ought to do; this let him, with true heart, do, and continue doing. The general issue will, as it has always done, rest well with a Higher Intelligence than ours. This day thou knowest ten commanded duties, seest in thy mind ten things which should be done for one that thou doest! *Do* one of them; this of itself will show thee ten others which can and shall be done.

THOMAS CARLYLE

88

Walk worthy of the Lord unto all pleasing, being fruitful in every good work, and increasing in the knowledge of God; strengthened with all might, according to His glorious power, unto all patience and longsuffering with joyfulness.

—COLOSSIANS i. 10–11

*I*t is not by regretting what is irreparable that true work is to be done, but by making the best of what we are. It is not by complaining that we have not the right tools, but by using well the tools we have.

FREDERICK WILLIAM ROBERTSON

Call unto me, and I will answer thee, and show thee great and mighty things which thou knowest not.

—JEREMIAH xxxiii. 3

*I*f you have any trial which seems intolerable, pray,—pray that it be relieved or changed. There is no harm in that. We may pray for anything, not wrong in itself, with perfect freedom, if we do not pray selfishly. One disabled from duty by sickness may pray for health, that he may do his work; or one hemmed in by internal impediments may pray for utterance, that he may serve better the truth and the right. . . .

But the answer to the prayer may be, as it was to Paul, not the removal of the thorn, but, instead, a growing insight into its meaning and value. The voice of God in our soul may show us, as we look up to Him, that His strength is enough to enable us to bear it.

JAMES FREEMAN CLARKE

God is our refuge and strength, a very present help in trouble. Therefore will not we fear, though the earth be removed, and though the mountains be carried into the midst of the sea.

—PSALM xlvi. 1–2

*L*earn to be as the angel, who could descend among the miseries of Bethesda without losing his heavenly purity or his perfect happiness. Gain healing from troubled waters. Make up your mind to the prospect of sustaining a certain measure of pain and trouble in your passage through life. By the blessing of God this will prepare you for it.

JOHN HENRY NEWMAN

Unless the Lord had been my help, my soul had almost dwelt in silence.

—PSALM xciv. 17

*T*he mind never puts forth greater power over itself than when, in great trials, it yields up calmly its desires, affections, interests to God. There are seasons when to be *still* demands immeasurably higher strength than to act. Composure is often the highest result of power. Think you it demands no power to calm the stormy elements of passion, to moderate the vehemence of desire, to throw off the load of dejection, to suppress every repining thought, when the dearest hopes are withered, and to turn the wounded spirit from dangerous reveries and wasting grief, to the quiet discharge of ordinary duties? Is there no power put forth, when a man, stripped of his property, of the fruits of a life's labors, quells discontent and gloomy forebodings, and serenely and patiently returns to the tasks which Providence assigns?

WILLIAM ELLERY CHANNING

The things which are impossible with men are possible with God.

—LUKE xviii. 27

I think I find most help in trying to look on all interruptions and hindrances to work that one has planned out for oneself as discipline, trials sent by God to help one against getting selfish over one's work. Then one can feel that perhaps one's true work one's work for God—consists in doing some trifling haphazard thing that has been thrown into one's day. It is not waste of time, as one is tempted to think, it is the most important part of the work of the day,—the part one can best offer to God. After such a hindrance, do not rush after the planned work; trust that the time to finish it will be given sometime, and keep a quiet heart about it.

ANNIE KEARY

Be merciful unto me, O God, be merciful unto me; for my soul trusteth in Thee: yea, in the shadow of Thy wings will I make my refuge, until these calamities be overpast.

—PSALM lvii. 1

God takes a thousand times more pains with us than the artist with his picture, by many touches of sorrow, and by many colors of circumstance, to bring man into the form which is the highest and noblest in His sight, if only we received His gifts and myrrh in the right spirit.

But when the cup is put away, and these feelings are stifled or unheeded, a greater injury is done to the soul than can ever be amended. For no heart can conceive in what surpassing love God giveth us this myrrh; yet this which we ought to receive to our soul's good, we suffer to pass by us in our sleepy indifference, and nothing comes of it. Then we come and complain: "Alas, Lord! I am so dry, and it is so dark within me!"

I tell thee, dear child, open thy heart to the pain, and it will do thee more good than if thou wert full of feeling and devoutness.

JOHN TAULER

Praise ye the Lord. Praise God in His sanctuary; praise Him in the firmament of His power.

Praise Him for his mighty acts: praise Him according to His excellent greatness.

Praise Him with the sound of the trumpet: praise Him with the psaltery and harp.

Praise Him with the timbrel and dance: praise Him with stringed instruments and organs.

Praise Him upon the loud cymbals: praise Him upon the high sounding cymbals.

Let everything that hath breath praise the Lord. Praise ye the Lord.

—PSALM cl